Book Title: "Transform Your Mindset: A Journey to Personal Growth"

I0409237

Book Chapters:

1. Understanding the Power of Mindset
2. The Role of Self-Awareness in Shaping Mindset
3. Overcoming Limiting Beliefs: Unleash Your Potential
4. Cultivating a Positive Mindset in a Negative World
5. The Science of Neuroplasticity: Rewiring Your Brain
6. Embracing Change and Resilience: A Mindset Shift
7. Goal Setting and the Mindset Connection
8. Nurturing Relationships through a Healthy Mindset
9. Mindset Mastery: Tools for Self-Development
10. Mindset and Success: Unleashing Your Full Potential
11. Mindfulness and Meditation: A Path to Clarity
12. Turning Failures into Stepping Stones with the Right Mindset
13. The Role of Gratitude in Shaping Your Mindset
14. Mindset and Emotional Intelligence: Finding Balance
15. Sustaining Your Transformed Mindset: A Lifelong Journey

Book Introduction:

In a world brimming with challenges and opportunities, your mindset becomes your most potent tool. "Transform Your Mindset: A Journey to Personal Growth" is an exploration of the incredible power that your thoughts, beliefs, and attitudes hold over the course of your life. This book delves deep into the art and science of reshaping your mindset to embrace positivity, conquer challenges, and foster personal growth.

More than just a collection of thoughts, your mindset serves as a lens through which you perceive and respond to the world around you. This book is your comprehensive guide to understanding and harnessing the potential of your mindset. By embracing the principles and practices outlined in these pages, you can embark on a transformative journey toward a more fulfilling, purpose-driven life.

Throughout these chapters, you'll explore the role of self-awareness in shaping your mindset, learn how to overcome limiting beliefs that have held you back, and discover the science behind rewiring your brain for success. From goal setting and resilience to the profound impact of gratitude and emotional intelligence, each chapter offers practical insights and actionable steps to help you achieve lasting change.

Are you ready to embark on a journey of self-discovery and personal growth? This book will equip you with the tools and wisdom to cultivate a mindset that not only empowers you to navigate life's challenges but also propels you towards your dreams and aspirations. Let's dive into the first chapter and begin this transformative adventure together.

Chapter 1: Understanding the Power of Mindset

Your mindset is the foundation upon which you build your life. It's the lens through which you view the world, interpret experiences, and make decisions. But what exactly is mindset, and how does it impact your life?

At its core, mindset refers to your attitudes, beliefs, and thought patterns. It's the mental framework that shapes your understanding of yourself, others, and the circumstances you encounter. A mindset can be either fixed or growth-oriented. A fixed mindset assumes that your abilities, intelligence, and traits are static, while a growth mindset embraces the idea that you can develop and improve through effort, learning, and perseverance.

The concept of mindset gained significant attention through the groundbreaking research of psychologist Carol Dweck. Her studies revealed that individuals with a growth mindset are more likely to embrace challenges, persist in the face of setbacks, and ultimately achieve higher levels of success. On the other hand, those with a fixed mindset tend to shy away from challenges and limit their potential due to a fear of failure.

So, why does mindset matter? Your mindset influences every aspect of your life. It affects your motivation, resilience, and ability to cope with adversity. It plays a pivotal role in your relationships, career, and overall well-being. By understanding and harnessing the power of mindset, you can take charge of your life's direction and unleash your full potential.

In the upcoming chapters, we will delve deeper into the nuances of mindset, exploring strategies to shift from a fixed mindset to a growth mindset. We will uncover the science behind neuroplasticity, the brain's remarkable ability to rewire itself, and how you can use this knowledge to reshape your thought patterns.

Are you ready to embark on a journey of self-transformation? As we explore the facets of mindset in the following chapters, keep in mind that the power to change begins with your thoughts. By cultivating a growth-oriented mindset, you're laying the groundwork for a life filled with purpose, resilience, and endless possibilities.

Chapter 2: The Role of Self-Awareness in Shaping Mindset

Self-awareness is the cornerstone of personal growth and a fundamental component of shaping your mindset. Understanding who you are, your strengths, weaknesses, values, and beliefs, is essential for cultivating a positive and growth-oriented mindset.

The Mirror of Reflection

Imagine self-awareness as a mirror that reflects your true self back to you. It's the ability to observe your thoughts, emotions, and behaviors without judgment, allowing you to gain insights into your patterns and tendencies. Self-awareness empowers you to recognize when you're operating from a fixed mindset and offers the opportunity to make a conscious shift towards a growth-oriented perspective.

The Journey Inward

Embarking on the journey of self-awareness requires a willingness to explore the depths of your being. This journey often involves self-reflection, introspection, and a commitment to honesty. Journaling, meditation, and seeking feedback from trusted individuals can all aid in uncovering the layers of your mindset.

Embracing Imperfections

One of the most powerful aspects of self-awareness is the acceptance of your imperfections. A growth mindset doesn't hinge on perfection but rather on progress. Embracing your flaws and understanding that they're part of your uniqueness enables you to approach challenges with resilience and an open mind.

Cultivating Self-Compassion

As you delve into self-awareness, remember to treat yourself with compassion. Developing self-compassion means acknowledging your struggles and treating yourself with the same kindness you would offer to a friend. This nurturing approach fosters a positive mindset that is supportive and encouraging.

The Ripple Effect

The benefits of self-awareness extend beyond your own growth. By understanding yourself better, you enhance your interactions with others. Empathy and understanding naturally flow from self-awareness, improving your relationships and creating a more positive environment around you.

As you continue on this journey of self-awareness, remember that it's a process, not a destination. Regular self-check-ins, moments of reflection, and a commitment to learning will enable you to shape a mindset that aligns with your aspirations. The upcoming chapters will delve deeper into practical techniques to enhance self-awareness and guide you towards a transformed mindset that paves the way for personal growth and success.

Chapter 3: Overcoming Limiting Beliefs - Unleash Your Potential

Our minds are often cluttered with limiting beliefs that hinder our progress and keep us from reaching our full potential. These beliefs, often ingrained from childhood or past experiences, create mental barriers that prevent us from embracing a growth-oriented mindset. In this chapter, we will explore how to identify and overcome these limiting beliefs to unlock your true potential.

The Power of Awareness

The first step in overcoming limiting beliefs is becoming aware of them. These beliefs are often so ingrained that they operate on autopilot, influencing our thoughts and actions without our conscious recognition. Through introspection and reflection, you can begin to identify these thoughts and question their validity.

Challenging Your Inner Critic

The inner critic is that nagging voice that tells you "you're not good enough" or "you'll never succeed." It's crucial to challenge this voice by asking for evidence that supports these beliefs. More often than not, you'll find that there's little to no substantial evidence, which weakens the grip of these negative thoughts.

Reframing Your Narrative

Once you've identified a limiting belief, work on reframing it. Transform negative self-talk into positive affirmations. For example, change "I can't do this" to "I can learn and improve with effort." By consciously changing the way you talk to yourself, you're rewiring your mindset for growth and resilience.

Embracing Failure as a Teacher

Limiting beliefs often stem from a fear of failure. Embracing failure as a natural part of the learning process is essential for a growth-oriented mindset. Instead of viewing failure as an endpoint, see it as a stepping stone towards improvement. Analyze what went wrong, learn from it, and apply those lessons moving forward.

Surrounding Yourself with Positivity

Your environment greatly influences your mindset. Surround yourself with people who support and uplift you. Seek out mentors, friends, or communities that encourage growth and positivity. Their perspectives and insights can help you challenge and overcome your limiting beliefs.

Taking Action Despite Fear

Action is a powerful antidote to limiting beliefs. The more you take action, the more evidence you gather that contradicts those beliefs. Stepping out of your comfort zone and facing your fears head-on will gradually diminish the hold that these beliefs have over you.

Cultivating a Growth Mindset

As you chip away at your limiting beliefs, you'll find that a growth mindset naturally starts to take root. Embracing challenges, seeking opportunities for learning, and persisting in the face of setbacks become second nature. Your mindset transforms from one of doubt and limitation to one of possibility and empowerment.

By dedicating yourself to overcoming your limiting beliefs, you're paving the way for a mindset that is aligned with your goals and dreams. Remember, you have the power to reshape your thoughts and beliefs, allowing you to unleash your untapped potential and embark on a journey of personal growth and transformation. The journey continues in the following chapters, where we'll explore strategies to cultivate a positive mindset in a world filled with negativity.

Chapter 4: Cultivating a Positive Mindset in a Negative World

In a world often filled with negativity, cultivating and maintaining a positive mindset is an invaluable asset. A positive mindset not only influences your emotional well-being but also shapes your experiences and interactions with others. This chapter delves into strategies for fostering a positive mindset, even in the face of challenges and negativity.

Mindful Awareness

Mindfulness is a powerful practice that can help you navigate the complexities of life with grace. By staying present in the moment and observing your thoughts without judgment, you can detach from negative thought patterns. Mindful awareness allows you to choose how you respond to situations, rather than reacting impulsively.

Gratitude as a Habit

Practicing gratitude is a proven method for shifting your focus from what's lacking to what's abundant in your life. Regularly taking time to reflect on the things you're grateful for can rewire your brain to seek out positivity. Gratitude also helps you appreciate small joys, fostering a more optimistic outlook.

Filtering Information

In an age of information overload, it's essential to filter the content you consume. Limit exposure to negative news and engage with sources that promote positivity and personal growth. The information you absorb significantly influences your mindset, so choose wisely.

Positive Self-Talk

Your internal dialogue plays a significant role in shaping your mindset. Replace self-criticism with self-encouragement. When faced with challenges, ask yourself, "What can I learn from this?" By reframing negative situations as opportunities for growth, you're fostering a positive mindset.

Surrounding Yourself with Positivity

The people you surround yourself with have a significant impact on your mindset. Build a supportive network of individuals who uplift and inspire you. Engaging in positive conversations and sharing experiences with like-minded individuals can reinforce your positive outlook.

Finding Meaning in Adversity

Challenges are inevitable, but they also provide opportunities for growth. Instead of dwelling on the negativity of a difficult situation, seek to uncover the lessons and silver linings. Viewing adversity as a chance to evolve and develop resilience contributes to a positive mindset.

Daily Positive Practices

Incorporate daily practices that boost your positivity. This could include meditation, affirmations, journaling, or acts of kindness. Consistency is key—small, positive actions accumulate over time, gradually shaping your mindset.

Embracing Setbacks as Learning Opportunities

A positive mindset doesn't mean avoiding setbacks; it means viewing them as part of the journey. Embrace setbacks as opportunities to learn and adapt. Each challenge you overcome strengthens your belief in your ability to handle adversity.

Cultivating a positive mindset is an ongoing practice that requires intention and effort. By implementing these strategies into your daily life, you're building a foundation of resilience, optimism, and empowerment. As we continue this journey of mindset transformation, the upcoming chapters will explore the science behind neuroplasticity and how you can leverage it to reshape your thought patterns and behaviors.

Chapter 5: The Science of Neuroplasticity - Rewiring Your Brain

Neuroplasticity, often referred to as the brain's "plasticity," is a revolutionary concept that has transformed our understanding of the brain's capabilities. This chapter delves into the science behind neuroplasticity and how you can harness its power to reshape your mindset and unlock your full potential.

The Brain's Adaptive Nature

Contrary to previous beliefs that the brain's structure was fixed in adulthood, neuroplasticity reveals that the brain has a remarkable ability to adapt and reorganize itself. It does so in response to learning, experience, and even injury. This means that you have the power to actively reshape your brain's neural pathways.

Use It or Lose It

Neuroplasticity operates on the principle of "use it or lose it." The brain strengthens connections that are frequently used while weakening those that are neglected. By engaging in activities that challenge your current mindset and encourage growth, you're directing your brain to form new pathways.

Learning Rewires the Brain

Learning is a prime example of neuroplasticity in action. When you learn a new skill or acquire knowledge, your brain creates new neural connections. The more you practice and reinforce what you've learned, the stronger these connections become. This process is at the heart of reshaping your mindset.

Harnessing Deliberate Practice

Deliberate practice is a technique that involves focused and mindful repetition of a skill or behavior. Through deliberate practice, you can deliberately mold your neural pathways to align with the mindset you're striving to cultivate. This technique is a powerful tool for personal growth.

Positive Affirmations and Visualization

Positive affirmations and visualization leverage the brain's plasticity to instill new beliefs and attitudes. By repeatedly affirming positive statements and vividly imagining your desired outcomes, you're programming your brain to accept these thoughts as reality.

Mindset and Stress Response

Neuroplasticity is closely linked to the brain's response to stress. Chronic stress can lead to negative changes in brain structure, affecting your mindset and overall well-being. Conversely, adopting a growth-oriented mindset can help mitigate the impact of stress on the brain.

Embracing Lifelong Learning

The brain's plasticity persists throughout life, making lifelong learning an essential component of maintaining a growth mindset. Continuously exposing yourself to new experiences, ideas, and challenges keeps your brain engaged and adaptable.

Practice Makes Progress

While neuroplasticity offers exciting possibilities for transformation, it's important to note that change takes time and consistent effort. Just as you would strengthen a muscle through consistent exercise, reshaping your mindset through neuroplasticity requires dedication and patience.

Understanding the science of neuroplasticity empowers you to take intentional steps towards rewiring your brain for growth and positive change. As we delve deeper into the chapters ahead, you'll learn practical techniques for leveraging neuroplasticity to overcome challenges and cultivate a mindset that propels you towards success and personal fulfillment.

Chapter 6: Embracing Change and Resilience - A Mindset Shift

Change is a constant in life, and the way you perceive and respond to change greatly influences your mindset. In this chapter, we explore the art of embracing change, building resilience, and adapting your mindset to navigate life's transitions with grace and confidence.

The Nature of Change

Change is an inevitable part of life's journey. Whether it's a career shift, a relationship change, or an unexpected event, your mindset plays a pivotal role in how you navigate and thrive in the face of change.

The Power of Adaptability

Adaptability is a hallmark of a growth-oriented mindset. Embracing change requires flexibility and the ability to adjust your perspectives and strategies. By remaining open to new possibilities, you can turn challenges into opportunities for growth.

Reframing Challenges as Opportunities

A shift in mindset can turn what seems like a setback into a stepping stone. When faced with challenges, ask yourself, "How can I grow from this experience?" Viewing obstacles as chances to learn and evolve strengthens your resilience.

Cultivating Resilience

Resilience is the ability to bounce back from adversity. It's closely tied to mindset—how you interpret and respond to difficulties. By fostering a growth-oriented mindset, you equip yourself with the tools to handle setbacks and emerge stronger.

Learning from Failure

Failure is not the end; it's a valuable lesson. A growth mindset enables you to see failure as a natural part of the journey. Analyzing what went wrong and applying those lessons to future endeavors propels you forward.

Embracing Uncertainty

Life is inherently uncertain, and embracing this uncertainty is a mindset shift in itself. Instead of fearing the unknown, adopt an attitude of curiosity and excitement. Embracing uncertainty opens the door to new experiences and opportunities.

The Role of Self-Compassion

During times of change, practicing self-compassion is crucial. Treat yourself with kindness and understanding, just as you would a close friend. Self-compassion provides a stable foundation as you navigate the shifting landscape of life.

Mindset and Growth Through Change

A growth-oriented mindset not only helps you navigate change but also facilitates personal growth during these times. By embracing change, adapting, and learning from the challenges it brings, you're continually evolving into the best version of yourself.

Your Mindset Toolbox

As you continue on your journey, consider these tools for embracing change and cultivating resilience:

- **Mindful Acceptance:** Acknowledge and accept change with mindfulness, rather than resistance.
- **Positive Self-Talk:** Encourage and reassure yourself during moments of uncertainty.
- **Flexibility:** Adapt your plans and perspectives as circumstances evolve.
- **Curiosity:** Approach change with a sense of curiosity and a desire to learn.
- **Learning Mindset:** View challenges as opportunities for growth and development.

By integrating these tools into your mindset, you're not only prepared to face change but also equipped to flourish and thrive amidst life's transitions. In the chapters ahead, we'll explore the intersection between mindset and goal setting, uncovering how your beliefs influence your journey towards success.

Chapter 7: Goal Setting and the Mindset Connection

Setting and pursuing goals is a fundamental aspect of personal growth and achievement. In this chapter, we'll delve into the intricate relationship between your mindset and goal setting, exploring how the way you approach goals can significantly impact your success.

The Importance of Clarity

A growth-oriented mindset begins with clarity. Clearly define your goals, both short-term and long-term. Clarity provides a roadmap for your journey, allowing you to channel your efforts effectively.

Embracing Challenges as Growth Opportunities

Goals often come with challenges, and a growth mindset positions you to embrace these challenges. Instead of avoiding difficulties, welcome them as opportunities for learning, improvement, and ultimately, achieving your goals.

Overcoming Self-Limiting Beliefs

Self-limiting beliefs can sabotage your goal-setting efforts. These beliefs often emerge as thoughts like "I'm not capable" or "I don't deserve success." A growth mindset empowers you to challenge and overcome these beliefs.

Persistence and Resilience

A growth mindset encourages persistence and resilience in the face of setbacks. Recognize that setbacks are part of the journey, and each one brings valuable lessons. Keep your eye on the bigger picture and maintain your commitment to your goals.

Embracing a Growth-Oriented Process

While achieving your goals is important, a growth-oriented mindset values the process just as much. The journey toward your goal is an opportunity for continuous learning, self-discovery, and personal development.

Celebrating Progress Along the Way

Acknowledging and celebrating your progress is crucial for maintaining motivation and a positive mindset. Break your larger goals into smaller milestones and take time to celebrate each achievement.

Mindset and Goal Visualization

Visualization is a powerful technique that aligns your mindset with your goals. Regularly visualize yourself successfully achieving your goals. This practice primes your mind for success and boosts your confidence.

Adaptability in Goal Setting

A growth-oriented mindset allows for adaptability in goal setting. As circumstances change, be open to adjusting your goals. Flexibility ensures that your goals remain relevant and attainable.

Empowering Affirmations

Incorporate positive affirmations that support your goals into your daily routine. These affirmations counteract negative self-talk and reinforce your belief in your ability to achieve your goals.

Mindset Mastery for Goal Achievement

By intertwining mindset mastery with your goal-setting journey, you're creating a potent formula for success. Your beliefs, attitudes, and perspectives significantly influence your ability to achieve your goals. As we continue exploring the connection between mindset and success in the chapters ahead, you'll discover techniques to amplify your mindset's impact on your journey to personal fulfillment and accomplishment.

Chapter 8: Nurturing Relationships through a Healthy Mindset

Your mindset doesn't only impact your personal growth; it also plays a pivotal role in your relationships. This chapter delves into how cultivating a healthy mindset can enhance your connections with others, fostering meaningful relationships that contribute to your overall well-being.

Empathy and Understanding

A growth-oriented mindset enhances your capacity for empathy and understanding. By recognizing that everyone is on their unique journey, you become more patient and compassionate in your interactions. This strengthens your relationships.

Open Communication

A positive mindset encourages open and honest communication. When you approach conversations with an open heart and mind, you create an environment where others feel heard and valued, leading to deeper connections.

Overcoming Conflict with Resilience

Conflicts are inevitable in any relationship. A growth mindset equips you with the resilience to navigate conflicts constructively. Instead of viewing conflicts as obstacles, approach them as opportunities for growth and improved understanding.

Cultivating Positivity in Relationships

Your mindset influences the energy you bring into your relationships. A positive outlook fosters positivity in interactions. By focusing on the strengths and positive qualities of others, you contribute to a harmonious atmosphere.

Supporting Others' Growth

A growth-oriented mindset not only supports your personal development but also encourages the growth of those around you. By believing in their potential and providing encouragement, you create a nurturing environment for everyone's growth.

Letting Go of Judgment

A judgmental mindset can strain relationships. Cultivating a nonjudgmental attitude allows you to accept others as they are, fostering an environment where people feel safe to be themselves.

Forgiveness and Healing

Forgiveness is a powerful tool for both personal growth and relationship nurturing. A growth mindset enables you to let go of grudges and work towards healing, both for yourself and your relationships.

Mindful Presence in Relationships

Being fully present in your interactions is a gift you give to others. Mindfulness in relationships enhances your connections by allowing you to genuinely listen, understand, and respond with empathy.

Fostering a Growth Culture

Cultivate a growth culture in your relationships by encouraging open dialogue about personal goals and challenges. Support each other's aspirations and celebrate achievements together.

Synergy of Growth Mindset and Relationships

As you nurture a growth-oriented mindset, you're simultaneously fostering healthy, fulfilling relationships. Your mindset influences your approach to communication, conflict resolution, and support, creating a positive feedback loop that benefits both you and those around you.

In the upcoming chapters, we'll explore the tools and techniques for mastering your mindset. By understanding the connection between mindset and emotional intelligence, you'll gain insights into regulating your emotions and enhancing your overall well-being, allowing you to navigate life's challenges with grace and resilience.

Chapter 9: Mindset Mastery - Tools for Self-Development

Mindset mastery is a continuous journey of self-awareness, growth, and transformation. This chapter introduces you to a toolkit of practical techniques that empower you to take charge of your mindset, unleashing your full potential and leading to personal development.

Self-Reflection

Regular self-reflection is a cornerstone of mindset mastery. Set aside time to assess your thoughts, beliefs, and reactions. Journaling or meditation can help you gain insights into your mindset patterns.

Affirmations

Positive affirmations are powerful tools for reshaping your thoughts and beliefs. Create a list of affirmations that align with the mindset you're cultivating. Repeat them daily to reinforce positive thinking.

Visualization

Visualization involves mentally rehearsing your goals and desired outcomes. By vividly imagining success, you're priming your mind for achievement and reinforcing your growth-oriented mindset.

Mindful Meditation

Mindful meditation cultivates present-moment awareness. Regular practice enhances your ability to observe your thoughts without judgment, allowing you to respond to situations with clarity and calmness.

Gratitude Practice

A gratitude practice shifts your focus from what's lacking to what's abundant in your life. Regularly expressing gratitude helps you maintain a positive mindset and fosters feelings of contentment.

Setting Intentional Goals

Setting intentional goals aligns your actions with your mindset. Create SMART (Specific, Measurable, Achievable, Relevant, Time-bound) goals that challenge you while remaining attainable.

Learning from Feedback

Feedback is a valuable source of growth. Approach feedback with an open mind, viewing it as an opportunity to learn and improve. A growth mindset welcomes constructive criticism.

Seeking Continuous Learning

A growth-oriented mindset thrives on learning. Continuously seek out new knowledge, experiences, and perspectives. Approach life with curiosity and a desire to expand your horizons.

Embracing Discomfort

Growth often involves stepping outside your comfort zone. Embrace discomfort as a sign of progress. Each challenge you tackle contributes to your mindset mastery.

Mindset Accountability Partners

Connect with others who are also focused on personal growth. Having mindset accountability partners provides mutual support, motivation, and a space for sharing insights and challenges.

Crafting Your Mindset Rituals

Create daily rituals that reinforce your growth-oriented mindset. Whether it's morning affirmations, evening reflections, or moments of mindfulness, consistent practices shape your mindset over time.

Progress Over Perfection

Remember that mindset mastery is a journey, not a destination. Embrace progress over perfection. Each small step you take contributes to your overall growth and development.

Your mindset toolkit empowers you to take proactive steps towards self-development and personal growth. As we delve into the upcoming chapters, you'll discover how emotional intelligence intertwines with your mindset, providing you with the tools to navigate emotions, build resilience, and foster deeper connections with yourself and others.

Chapter 10: Mindset and Success - Unleashing Your Full Potential

Success is a culmination of mindset, effort, and opportunity. In this chapter, we explore the intricate connection between your mindset and achieving success, as well as the strategies you can employ to unlock your full potential and accomplish your goals.

The Mindset-Success Link

Your mindset significantly influences your approach to success. A growth-oriented mindset positions you to embrace challenges, persist in the face of setbacks, and view failures as stepping stones towards your goals.

Setting Bold Goals

A growth mindset empowers you to set bold, ambitious goals. These goals stretch your capabilities and motivate you to reach higher levels of achievement. Your mindset shapes your belief in your ability to achieve these goals.

Embracing the Journey

Success isn't solely about reaching the destination; it's about embracing the journey. A growth-oriented mindset values the process, learning, and growth that occur along the way. Each step forward contributes to your success.

Overcoming Imposter Syndrome

Imposter syndrome, the feeling of being a fraud despite evidence of competence, can hinder your path to success. A growth mindset helps you overcome imposter syndrome by recognizing your worth and capabilities.

Cultivating a Positive Work Ethic

A growth-oriented mindset encourages a positive work ethic. You approach your tasks with enthusiasm, focus, and determination. Challenges become opportunities to showcase your dedication and perseverance.

Handling Criticism and Feedback

Success often invites criticism and feedback. A growth mindset allows you to accept constructive feedback gracefully and use it to improve. Instead of viewing criticism as a setback, see it as a chance to grow.

Navigating Fear of Failure

Fear of failure can paralyze your progress. A growth mindset helps you navigate this fear by viewing failure as a natural part of the journey. Each failure is a lesson that brings you closer to success.

Resilience in the Face of Setbacks

Setbacks are inevitable on the path to success. A growth-oriented mindset equips you with the resilience to bounce back from setbacks. You're more likely to persevere when you believe in your ability to overcome challenges.

Celebrating Achievements

A growth mindset celebrates achievements along the way. Recognizing your progress and accomplishments boosts your confidence and motivation, propelling you towards even greater success.

Creating a Success Mindset

Cultivating a success mindset involves aligning your thoughts, beliefs, and actions with your aspirations. By embracing challenges, staying focused on your goals, and maintaining a positive outlook, you're creating the mindset necessary for achieving the success you desire.

In the chapters ahead, we'll explore the profound impact of mindfulness and meditation on your mindset. These practices can enhance your emotional intelligence, help you manage stress, and foster a deeper sense of self-awareness, all of which contribute to your overall success and well-being.

Chapter 11: Mindfulness and Meditation - A Path to Clarity

Mindfulness and meditation are transformative practices that enhance your mindset and overall well-being. In this chapter, we delve into the power of mindfulness and meditation, exploring how they cultivate clarity, emotional resilience, and a deeper connection with yourself.

The Essence of Mindfulness

Mindfulness is the art of being fully present in the moment. It involves observing your thoughts, emotions, and sensations without judgment. Practicing mindfulness enables you to navigate life with greater clarity and awareness.

Emotional Regulation through Mindfulness

Mindfulness empowers you to regulate your emotions. By acknowledging your feelings without immediately reacting, you create space for thoughtful responses rather than impulsive reactions. This emotional intelligence enhances your interactions and decision-making.

Cultivating Inner Peace

In a fast-paced world, mindfulness offers a sanctuary of inner peace. Regular mindfulness practice calms the mind, reduces stress, and fosters a sense of tranquility that extends to all aspects of your life.

Mindfulness and Self-Compassion

Mindfulness is intertwined with self-compassion. By observing your thoughts and emotions without judgment, you're cultivating a compassionate relationship with yourself. This self-compassion supports a positive self-image and a growth-oriented mindset.

The Power of Meditation

Meditation is a focused practice that trains your mind and enhances your awareness. Through meditation, you're strengthening your mental muscles, improving your ability to concentrate, and fostering mindfulness in daily life.

Developing Resilience through Meditation

Meditation builds resilience by increasing your capacity to handle stress and adversity. Regular practice rewires your brain, promoting a calmer response to challenges and a greater ability to bounce back from setbacks.

Mindfulness in Action

Mindful living extends beyond formal practice. Engage in everyday activities mindfully, from eating to interacting with others. This practice enhances your appreciation for the present moment and deepens your connection to life.

Meditation Techniques

Various meditation techniques cater to different preferences and needs. Guided meditation, focused attention, loving-kindness meditation, and body scan are just a few approaches you can explore.

A Holistic Transformation

The synergy of mindfulness and meditation nurtures your mindset and well-being. As you cultivate mindfulness and integrate meditation into your routine, you're undergoing a holistic transformation that influences your thoughts, emotions, behaviors, and relationships.

Mindful Mindset Mastery

Mindfulness and meditation are integral to mastering your mindset. By incorporating these practices into your daily life, you're enhancing your self-awareness, emotional intelligence, and ability to navigate challenges with grace. As we approach the final chapters, we'll explore the role of gratitude in shaping your mindset, as well as the intersection between mindset and emotional intelligence.

Chapter 12: The Gratitude Mindset - Cultivating Positivity

Gratitude is a powerful force that can transform your mindset and outlook on life. In this chapter, we explore the concept of the gratitude mindset, its impact on your well-being, and how practicing gratitude can foster a positive and growth-oriented perspective.

The Gratitude Mindset

A gratitude mindset involves consistently focusing on the positive aspects of life and appreciating the abundance around you. By shifting your attention to what you have rather than what you lack, you cultivate a positive outlook.

Rewiring Your Brain with Gratitude

Practicing gratitude triggers positive neurochemical reactions in your brain. It releases dopamine and serotonin, enhancing your mood and fostering a sense of contentment and well-being.

Gratitude's Effect on Emotional Resilience

Gratitude contributes to emotional resilience by helping you manage stress and negative emotions. When you acknowledge and appreciate the good in your life, you build a reservoir of positivity to draw from during challenging times.

The Ripple Effect of Gratitude

The benefits of gratitude extend beyond your personal well-being. Expressing gratitude towards others strengthens your relationships, fosters a sense of community, and uplifts the spirits of those around you.

Gratitude Practices

There are various ways to integrate gratitude into your daily life:

- **Gratitude Journaling:** Write down three things you're grateful for each day.
- **Mindful Gratitude:** Savor positive moments and experiences as they occur.
- **Expressing Thanks:** Verbally express gratitude to others and let them know you appreciate them.

The Gratitude Mindset and Mindfulness

The gratitude mindset and mindfulness are intertwined. Both practices anchor you in the present moment and enhance your ability to appreciate life's simple pleasures.

Cultivating Gratitude in Adversity

Practicing gratitude during challenging times can be particularly transformative. Even in difficult situations, there are silver linings and lessons to be learned. Shifting your focus to these aspects fosters resilience and growth.

The Growth-Oriented Gratitude Mindset

A gratitude mindset aligns seamlessly with a growth-oriented perspective. By appreciating the progress you've made, the lessons you've learned, and the people who've supported you, you reinforce your commitment to personal development.

The Gift of Gratitude

Cultivating a gratitude mindset is a gift you give to yourself and those around you. By consistently acknowledging the positive aspects of life, you're shaping a mindset that radiates positivity, fosters resilience, and nurtures personal growth.

As we approach the final chapter, we'll explore the culmination of these concepts—how emotional intelligence and a growth-oriented mindset combine to create a foundation for a fulfilling, purpose-driven life.

Chapter 13: Emotional Intelligence and Mindset - The Ultimate Synergy

Emotional intelligence (EI) and a growth-oriented mindset are two powerful forces that, when combined, create a harmonious and purpose-driven life. In this chapter, we delve into the synergy between EI and mindset, exploring how they amplify each other and contribute to your overall well-being.

Understanding Emotional Intelligence

Emotional intelligence encompasses the ability to recognize, understand, manage, and effectively use your emotions. It also involves empathizing with the emotions of others and managing interpersonal relationships with empathy and wisdom.

Emotional Intelligence and Self-Awareness

A growth-oriented mindset begins with self-awareness, a key component of emotional intelligence. By understanding your emotions, triggers, and patterns, you're better equipped to align your mindset with your goals.

Emotional Regulation and Mindset

Emotional intelligence enhances your ability to regulate your emotions. When faced with challenges or setbacks, emotional regulation prevents impulsive reactions and enables you to respond thoughtfully, in line with your growth-oriented mindset.

Empathy and Connection

Empathy is a hallmark of emotional intelligence. Cultivating empathy enhances your relationships and your growth mindset. Understanding others' perspectives fosters open communication and encourages collaboration.

Social Skills and Collaboration

Effective social skills are an essential aspect of emotional intelligence. Building and maintaining relationships, resolving conflicts, and collaborating are all enhanced by a growth-oriented mindset and emotional intelligence.

Mindfulness and Emotional Intelligence

Mindfulness, a practice that enhances emotional intelligence, aligns seamlessly with a growth-oriented mindset. Both practices involve present-moment awareness, self-compassion, and a nonjudgmental attitude.

The Power of Resilience

Resilience, a product of both emotional intelligence and a growth-oriented mindset, enables you to bounce back from challenges and setbacks. The ability to manage your emotions, remain adaptable, and view setbacks as opportunities fuels your resilience.

Building a Purpose-Driven Life

The synergy of emotional intelligence and mindset creates a foundation for a purpose-driven life. By understanding your emotions, maintaining a growth-oriented perspective, and nurturing relationships, you're fostering a life rich in fulfillment and meaning.

A Holistic Approach

Emotional intelligence and a growth-oriented mindset are integral to holistic well-being. As you continue to develop both aspects, you're building a strong foundation for personal growth, success, and a fulfilling life.

In the final chapter, we'll explore the culmination of these concepts—how they converge to shape your purpose-driven life and leave a lasting impact on your personal journey and the lives of those around you.

Chapter 14: Living a Purpose-Driven Life

A purpose-driven life is the culmination of a growth-oriented mindset, emotional intelligence, and a commitment to personal development. In this final chapter, we explore how these concepts intersect to shape a life that is meaningful, impactful, and aligned with your true potential.

Defining Your Purpose

Discovering your purpose involves aligning your passions, values, and strengths. A growth-oriented mindset empowers you to explore new possibilities, adapt to changing circumstances, and embrace the journey of self-discovery.

Embracing Emotional Fulfillment

Emotional intelligence enables you to recognize what truly brings you joy and fulfillment. By understanding your emotions and seeking experiences that resonate with your authentic self, you're creating a life that aligns with your values and desires.

Navigating Challenges with Resilience

A purpose-driven life doesn't exempt you from challenges; it equips you to face them with resilience and determination. Your growth-oriented mindset and emotional intelligence allow you to find lessons in adversity and emerge stronger.

Impacting Others through Connection

The intersection of mindset and emotional intelligence fosters meaningful connections with others. By empathizing, communicating effectively, and collaborating, you're not only enriching your life but also making a positive impact on those around you.

Cultivating Gratitude and Contentment

Gratitude, a growth-oriented mindset, and emotional intelligence work harmoniously to cultivate contentment. You appreciate the journey, acknowledge your progress, and find joy in the present moment, contributing to a sense of fulfillment.

Creating a Legacy of Growth

A purpose-driven life leaves a legacy of growth, resilience, and compassion. By embodying a growth-oriented mindset and emotional intelligence, you inspire others to embark on their own journeys of self-discovery and personal development.

The Ongoing Journey

Living a purpose-driven life is an ongoing journey that evolves as you do. As you continue to nurture your growth-oriented mindset and emotional intelligence, you're continually refining your purpose, expanding your impact, and deepening your fulfillment.

Your Purpose-Driven Blueprint

Craft a purpose-driven blueprint that integrates mindset and emotional intelligence:

- **Set Meaningful Goals:** Align your goals with your purpose and values.
- **Practice Mindfulness:** Cultivate present-moment awareness in your endeavors.
- **Prioritize Relationships:** Foster connections based on empathy and understanding.
- **Embrace Challenges:** View challenges as opportunities for growth and learning.
- **Celebrate Progress:** Acknowledge your achievements and milestones along the way.

By weaving these elements together, you're creating a tapestry of a purpose-driven life that is uniquely yours.

Conclusion

The journey of cultivating a growth-oriented mindset, nurturing emotional intelligence, and living a purpose-driven life is both transformative and fulfilling. This exploration of concepts and practices has equipped you with the tools to embark on this journey with intention and dedication. As you move forward, remember that your mindset is a powerful force that shapes your reality—embrace it, nurture it, and let it guide you towards a life of purpose, growth, and lasting impact.

Epilogue: A Lifelong Pursuit

The journey you've embarked upon—of cultivating a growth-oriented mindset, developing emotional intelligence, and living a purpose-driven life—is not a destination but a lifelong pursuit. As you continue on this path, remember that growth is a continuous process, and every experience, challenge, and success contributes to your evolution.

Embrace each day with the intention to learn, adapt, and expand your horizons. Approach setbacks as opportunities for learning, view challenges as stepping stones, and celebrate your progress along the way. Your mindset is the compass guiding you through life's twists and turns, shaping your responses, decisions, and interactions.

Cultivate mindfulness as a companion on your journey—a practice that keeps you grounded, present, and attuned to your inner self. The synergy of emotional intelligence and a growth-oriented mindset enhances your self-awareness, enriches your relationships, and fuels your pursuit of a purpose-driven life.

Your impact is not limited to your personal growth; it ripples out to touch the lives of those around you. By embodying these principles, you inspire others to explore their potential, overcome challenges, and lead lives that align with their values and aspirations.

As you navigate the chapters of your life, remember that your story is a testament to your commitment to growth, resilience, and authenticity. May your journey be filled with discovery, transformation, and the fulfillment that comes from living a purpose-driven life.

www.ingramcontent.com/pod-product-compliance
Lightning Source LLC
Chambersburg PA
CBHW050530290526
45786CB00007B/2763